THE NEW SOLUTION TO THE PROBLEM OF INFLATION

Help get rid of the spiral cycle: Money supply – Inflation - Recession

I0397098

SUMMARY

Address the problem of inflation by putting money into circulation directly through commercial enterprises in order to always respect the principle of: "Money is only put into circulation when the society has acquired materials and goods as control objects to ensure value for money; And when such materials and goods are no longer available, they are sold for consumption, the money from the circulation must be recovered. "

So we will always have a balance in value between Goods and Money in a dynamically growing economy, and inflation will be automatically suppressed. We will get out of the spiral cycle: money supply - inflation - recession. The value of the national currency will always be solid and stable.

This solution will help countries suffering from high inflation such as Venezuela, Zimbabwe, ... control the balance of value of goods and money in the market economy of their country, from which will control and gradually will eliminate inflation.

This solution can also help countries want to convert the economy from a centrally planned economy (such as Cuba, North Korea, ...) to a market economy safely, effectively, and avoid causing major shocks (due to rising prices) in the economy, because of the control the balance of value of goods and money in the economy of their country.

This solution will help countries in the world to perfect the market economy, helping countries get rid of the spiral cycle: money supply-inflation-degradation. The market economy of the countries will grow as fast as it can without suffering inflation or deflation dragging it back anymore.

I would like to introduce the book "THE NEW SOLUTION TO THE PROBLEM OF INFLATION" to you.

Nguyen Cao Dung

Copyright reserved. Please quote the source and author's name.

PAPER MONEY UNDER GENERAL MERCHANDISE STANDARD AND INCONVERTIBLE PAPER MONEY

As you know, paper money under the gold standard is banknote that replaced for gold coins that people deposit (gold coins) at the bank. The person who has this kind of banknote can arrive to the place that the banknote were put into circulation (the issuing bank) in exchange for a quantity of gold that corresponds to the value recorded on the banknote at any time they need. The paper money regime under the gold standard is the hedge against inflation, which prevents the government from printing paper money arbitrarily.

Now expanding more, we will expand and develop the paper money regime under the gold standard into the paper money regime under **general merchandise standard** (the gold merchandise standard expanded) for all kinds of goods on the market (including gold). We will take all kinds of goods available on the market (including gold) as the basis for monetary, as the basis for putting money into circulation. According to the paper money regime under the general merchandise standard, the person who has this kind of banknote can arrive to the place that the banknote were put into circulation (at commercial businesses) in exchange for a amount of goods that corresponds to the value recorded on the banknote at any time they need.

Gold is a precious metal, rare and not much in society. Meanwhile, the population is increasing in society, the economy is growing, produce goods more and more and diverse, thus requiring money - intermediate means of exchange - also need to have money more and more to cater to the needs of exchanging goods for every people in society. But gold is not much, so the **convertible** paper money regime under the gold standard could not ensure sufficient quantity of money necessary in circulation. Therefore, it has caused a lack of money, lack of means of exchange of goods, caused stagnation of goods, congestion in the circulation and exchange of goods, leading to stagnation of production and inhibits the development of economy, caused recession and economic crisis.

The paper money regime under the general merchandise standard will overcome the disadvantages of the gold [merchandise] standard, the money - intermediate means of exchange, will not be short of money in circulation. Thus the exchange of goods for every people in society will be easy, fast, smooth, and not be congested. Goods produced will no longer be stagnant due to lack of money in circulation (lack of liquidity - everyone has the demand for commodities in the market but do not have money to buy), the manufacturer will no longer stalled and stagnated. The paper money regime under the general merchandise standard will help avoid and prevent recession and economic crisis.

The paper money under the general merchandise standard is the [merchandise] convertible paper money, it has the ability to convert paper money into the merchandises at any time at the place where it is put into circulation (at the commercial enterprise). It is not the inconvertible paper money. It always has the goods at the place where it is put into circulation (at commercial businesses) as evidence to ensure value for money. As also the paper money regime under the [merchandise] gold standard, the paper money regime under the general merchandise standard is the hedge against inflation, it prevents, does not allow the Government from arbitrarily printing out paper money to invest, spend or lend for investment, spending and therefore will not cause inflation.

Meanwhile, the inconvertible paper money is the kind of money forced and compulsory circulated, people can not take the paper money to where it was put into circulation (central banks - the issuing bank and put money into circulation) in exchange for a gold or silver or any other commodity. The inconvertible paper money does not get the guaranteed value of gold, silver or any other commodity in where it was put into circulation.

The inconvertible paper money regime has not prevented the Government subjectively (leading to arbitrary) from printing of paper money to invest, spend or lending to invest, spend, thus causing inflation. The inconvertible paper money regime (which is now used in the world) itself is the source that produces inflation, produces uncertainty, instability, causing anxiety, confusion, and caused economic crisis, financial, monetary, within each country, region, as well as on a global scale.

CHAPTER 1

THE CAUSE OF INFLATION

So far, in Vietnam as in other countries around the world, inflation is still a threat frequently to the development of the economy. Inflation makes the life of each person adding anxiety and thoughts to deal with, reduces the quality of life of low-income people, affects everyone in society. The impact of inflation makes reduce the purchasing power of the poor and makes increase inequality of income, delays the economic relationships related to buying and selling, affects negatively on the growth of the economy.

The cause of inflation is mainly due to the government printed paper money to spend to offset the deficit in the budget, and / or due to the government/Central Bank printed paper money to the other economic institutions borrowing to invest in manufacturing, basic construction, ... but the government does not have the corresponding object as evidence to ensure value for money. To better understand why there is inflation, we first need to study what the money (banknotes) really is.

1.1. PAPER MONEY IS ONLY A SPECIAL TYPE OF COUPON

Considering in the centrally planned economies of countries have used coupons many years ago (such as Vietnam, Cuba, North Korea...), each type of coupons will be issued for each respective type of goods. On each coupon recorded clearly quantity and type of goods that it represents. Owners with these coupons will receive quantity and type of goods corresponding recorded on the coupons. The more the coupons, the more likely they are to get more quantity and variety of goods. After people receive the goods, the coupons will be destroyed (shredded) away. Such cancellations will create waste and costly to society, many types of coupons were issued and then destroyed again after people received the goods. We can improve these coupons so that they can be re-used to avoid wasting society.

Digitize the types of coupons

The coupons are issued corresponding to each type of product, goods that are carried away for distribution.

The quantity of each type of coupons issued correspond to the volume of each type of goods to be carried away for distribution.

The coupons are issued when there are goods in society, and the coupons are distributed to the members and the organization in society.

In social there are kinds of goods: A, B, C, D, E, F, ...

with the volume: Ma, Mb, Mc, Md, Me, Mf, ...

We follow each step below:

We arrange the goods taken distribution by value from low to high.

Society has n types of goods, there will be n types of coupons.

Each coupon released corresponds to each volume (quantity) of the type of goods which it represents.

Each item in the i position with Mi units of volume will also release the same number Mi of coupons corresponding.

The total number of coupons will be issued will correspond to the total volume (quantity) of products, goods will be taken and distributed to everyone in society.

We do not need to specify the name and type of goods, products on the coupons anymore. We arrange the items by value from low to high, so that the value of the goods will be compared, identified and set out the specific numbers (expressed low or high values of the goods). We will specify the value number (value of the goods) on the coupon instead of specifying the name of goods on the coupon. The value numbers (value of the goods) recorded on the coupons are positive integers or decimal (eg 1; 2.15; 10; 25.55; 100; 312; ...).

To get the right products, goods that they really need, people now can exchange the coupons for each other, but the exchange still has some inconvenience due to the value numbers expressing the value of goods on the coupons are usually decimal, cause certain difficulties for exchanges. We found that the total value of coupons issued will be equal to the total value of goods in society. With the value numbers shown on the coupons are often decimal, cause some difficulties for the exchange of the coupons. So can we improve further?

Unify the types of Coupons

We will release a new type of coupon from which it can represent all kinds of goods in society, with positive integers recorded on some new coupons (eg: 1; 2, 5, 10, 20, 50, 100, 500, 1000, ...), and the decimal recorded on some other new coupons (eg: 0.1, 0.2, 0.5, 0 , 01, 0.02, 0.05, ...). The combination of the new types of coupons will not represent for any particular items at all that it will represent for all kinds of goods in society.

The total value of the new coupons are released, of course, must be equal to the total value of the goods will be distributed to everyone in society.

Who wants to exchange the coupons for a particular item with decimal values (eg, item X (31.95 value) for example), they can exchange 01 coupon (50) and receive 01 coupon (10), 01 coupon (5), 03 coupons (1), and 01 coupon (0,05) and get X item (50 - 31.95 = 18.05 = 10 + 5 + (1 x 3) + 0.05). Because everyone has some simple mathematical knowledge, and the types of products and goods are compared and identified (by specific value numbers), the exchange of new coupons for goods will be easier and more convenient.

After everyone has received the goods, the coupons will be collected on. These coupons will not need to be destroyed after being collected again due to its conveniences, and the coupons absolutely can be easily re-used for the next time. The types of special coupons with its using values especially important, so it is necessary to have a functional agency and authorized by the Government to authenticate, validate and manage all kinds of the coupons.

After a process of improvement in rather complex above, we found that the coupons have become identical and coincide with today's paper money. This special coupon is paper money. Banknote in essence is a kind of special coupons, it represents all kinds of goods in society and it is used and re-use many times in society.

Coupons are issued when goods are available in society. Paper money is just a special kind of coupons, so paper money also should be only issued and put into circulation when there are goods available in society. Identifying clearly, what paper money actually is, will help us understand thoroughly more about currency, thereby issuing and using currency more scientifically, avoid causing undue disturbance (inflation) that should not be had in society.

1.2. WHY THERE IS INFLATION

Considering in the economy of commodity production, production meets sufficiently consumer demand for the whole society. We divide the economy into four production areas:

Area 1: Area produces productive assets (TLSX)

Area 2: Area produces materials

Area 3: Area produces fuels, and

Area 4: Area produces consumption materials (TLTD).

We call:

C   :   The total value of productive assets produced in a period.

Ng   :   The total value of materials produced in a period.

Nl   :   The total value of the fuel produced in a period.

P   :   The total value of consumption materials produced in a period.

V   :   The total by money earnings of workers and profits of the business in a period

Area 1: The production activities in the sector producing productive assets with the participation of machinery and equipment (C1), materials (Ng1), fuel (Nl1), labor and the cooperation of people in the business (V1) produce productive assets (C) sufficient for the whole society. In terms of value, we can express in the following mathematical formula:

$$C1 + Ng1 + Nl1 + V1 = C \qquad (1)$$

Area 2: The production activities in the sector producing materials with the participation of machinery and equipment (C2), materials (Ng2), fuel (Nl2), labor and the cooperation of people in the business (V2) generated materials (Ng) sufficient for the whole society. In terms of value, we can express in the following mathematical formula:

$$C2 + Ng2 + NI2 + V2 = Ng \quad (2)$$

Area 3: The production activities in the sector producing fuels with the participation of machinery and equipment (C3), materials (Ng3), fuel (NI3), labor and the cooperation of the people in the business (V3) to create fuel (NI) sufficient for the whole society. In terms of value, we can express in the following mathematical formula:

$$C3 + Ng3 + NI3 + V3 = NI \quad (3)$$

Area 4: The production activities in the sector producing consumption materials with the participation of machinery (C4), materials (Ng4), fuel (NI4), labor and the cooperation of people in the business (V4) generated consumption materials (P) sufficient for the whole society. In terms of value, we can express in the following mathematical formula:

$$C4 + Ng4 + NI4 + V4 = P \quad (4)$$

With production fully meets the demand of the whole society, we get:

$$C1 \ + C2 \ + C3 \ + C4 \ = C \quad (5)$$

$$Ng1 + Ng2 + Ng3 + Ng4 = Ng \quad (6)$$

$$NI1 + NI2 + NI3 + NI4 = NI \quad (7)$$

Plus: (1) + (2) + (3) + (4)

And by: (5), (6), (7)

We inferred:

$$V1 + V2 + V3 + V4 = P \quad (8)$$

Or $V = P$ (9)

The division of the economy into four production areas as above only for the purpose of simplifying the calculation model, we can actually divide the economy into more than four areas, but we finally still get: $V = P$ (9)

That means Total earnings of workers and profits of the business in one period is always equal to the total value of consumer materials produced in that period.

This proves that: If we (the whole society) live and spend on our own incomes, we (the whole society) will always have enough goods to buy and the prices of goods will not be increased.

The division of the economy into the different production areas are relative only. Review on the whole social perspective, we find that the whole society producing is for the whole society consuming.

Now if the Government printed more amount of money (t) to spend on, and the Government also had no plans to recover the amount of money (t), this will make the total income fund [expressed by money] of the whole society will increase, and will be $(V + t)$, but the volume of goods of the whole society remains still unchanged, so will put pressure makes rising prices of goods, causing inflation.

In summary,

1. If the government printed money to spend, then inflation occurs is inevitable.

2. Expand more:

Only credit growth by printing money to finance consumption, basic construction, etc., is cause inflation. And the growth of credit by printing money for commercial development loans to facilitate the exchange of goods for each other easier and more convenient, does not cause inflation. The credit growth, through allowing the commercial businesses borrowing money (from the source of issuance money) to make purchasing and selling, because always get the goods as evidence [to put money into circulation], always ensure the balance of value between Goods and Money, so does not cause inflation.

3- The amount of foreign currency remitted by overseas Vietnamese to their country each year will be balanced against the volume of imported goods from that amount of foreign currency, so it will not cause inflation.

But, if the State Bank / Central Bank issues money to buy that amount of foreign currency to increase national foreign exchange reserves, thereby putting money into circulation in society and letting other people spend it, not using that amount of foreign currency to import a volume of goods with corresponding value to ensure the balance of value between the Goods and Money in the domestic market, will cause inflation.

The second conclusion above is very important, it makes a big difference between this anti-inflation solution of us and other anti-inflation measures developed by other authors. This is the launching point for whole our solutions in solving the inflation problem.

CHAPTER 2
THE SOLUTION TO THE PROBLEM OF INFLATION

2.1. THE INITIAL VIEWPOINTS

Our research direction derives from the following perspectives:

- Whether gold coins or paper money, MONEY with its nominal value determined and recorded by the Government on the surface of the money; and goods with its real value identified and recognized by society, money is just the intermediate objects to help for the exchange of products of people for each others in society being easy, fast and convenient, through the buying and selling activities in the market.

- The money put into circulation must always achieve a balance of value between goods and money in circulation process in society in order to not cause inflation.

Money is only an intermediary to facilitate the exchange of products of people in the society through trading activities in the market. Having money is must having goods to buy. There should be no cases having money but having no goods to buy made pressure caused inflation. So, money is only put into circulation when there are materials and goods available as evidences to ensure the value of money; and when the materials, goods are no longer available, the evidences have been sold, consumed, the money from the circulation must be collected on. In other words, money put into circulation must always achieve a balance of value between goods and money in the circulation in society so as not to cause inflation.

- Money put into circulation must rely on commercial enterprises to always achieve a balance of value between goods and money, not to cause inflation.

Commercial businesses are places where buying and selling activities take place, where goods are stored for the whole society, regardless of whether they are wholesale or retail businesses.

Commercial enterprises are places where goods are stored for the whole society, where people exchange goods for each other in the society, where they really hold the goods. Therefore, the introduction of money into circulation must rely on commercial enterprises. Money is put into circulation through the commercial enterprises will always have materials, goods (which commercial enterprises buy) as evidence to ensure value for money. Money is put into circulation when commercial businesses buy goods, and when the goods are sold, the money from circulation is collected. So creating a balance in terms of value between Goods and Money, eliminating inflation.

In our approach to solving problem of inflation, we will firstly come up with a standardized approach to putting money into circulation so as to consistently create a balance in terms of value between Goods and Money in the economy in order to not cause inflation. Then, based on the standardized approach have found, we will adjust the current imbalance of value between the Goods and Money to the state of equilibrium according to the plan mentioned to solve definitively the inflation.

Create a balance of value between Goods and Money and always maintain a balance of value in Goods and Money in the economy always moving and developing, that is the viewpoint throughout our whole solution in solving the problem of inflation. The relationship in value between the Goods and Money is balanced, the most important balanced relationship of the economy is established, inflation will be eliminated and the economy will grow as fast as it can.

2.2. PLAN A: PUTTING MONEY INTO CIRCULATION RELY ON COMMERCIAL ENTERPRISES

To simplify the problem, we assume that in society there are products but not money. We will put money into circulation to help people exchange products for each other easily, quickly and conveniently.

2.2.1. Purpose and requirements

• Purpose:

Money is put into circulation to make as intermediate objects to help the exchange of products of people being easy, fast and convenient relying on the buying and selling activities in society. Money is put into circulation to help the operation and the development of economy, not to cause inflation.

• Requirements:

Money put into circulation must achieve a balance of value between Goods and Money:

- Money put into circulation must have materials, goods available as evidence (for controlling) to ensure the value for money.

- When the control objects are no longer available, when such supplies and goods have been exchanged or consumed, the money from the circulation must be collected.

2.2.2. Objects in order to money being put into circulation

Money being put into circulation is to assist the exchange of products of people together in society being easy, fast and convenient.

So the objects in order to money being put into circulation in society are all kinds of products already in society, be exchanged and potentially exchanged (sold) on the market. Money is only put into circulation when there are goods available in society and those goods must have the ability to be exchanged on the market, not allow printing money to spend, if the goods are inability to be exchanged on the market, the commercial enterprises are not allowed to put money into circulation.

And then, when the goods are no longer available in the society, the goods have been consumed, the money from the circulation must be received.

In other words, commercial enterprises are only permitted to use the money provided (from the source of issuance money) for trading (buy and sell only), in addition, are no longer allowed to use the money provided for any other purpose.

2.2.3. Method of putting money into circulation

The method of putting money into circulation through commercial enterprises is carried out as follows:

- First, money is printed out and provided to commercial businesses in the form of loans. Commercial businesses will regulate and put money into circulation through the trading operations of buying and selling of them.

The Central Bank will print money and provide money to commercial banks. Subsequently, commercial banks will provide back to commercial businesses in the form of loans. The commercial business use the proceeds of this loan only for the purposes of trading in buying and selling in order to put money into circulation in society, in addition, no longer allowed to use the proceeds of this loan for any other purpose.

Commercial businesses must be solely responsible for their business operations of buying and selling. If having profits they shall enjoy, and if having loss they have to compensate by their income expressed in money.

The Central Bank together with Commercial Banks will manage and control the introduction of money into circulation by commercial enterprises to ensure that commercial enterprises use their loans for the right purpose. The cases of loans must ensure that the loans are repaid.

- Then, the money from the commercial enterprises will be put into circulation relying on the **purchase** of goods of commercial enterprises. Commercial businesses need to pay the seller immediately after receiving the goods. It is necessary to do so to fully meet the monetary needs of society, to ensure that money is not lacking in circulation. By action paid money to the seller, which money from commercial enterprises are put into circulation in society.

We always have:

$$\begin{array}{ccc} \text{The total value} & & \text{The total value of} \\ \text{of money put} & & \text{materials and} \\ \text{into circulation} & = & \text{goods purchased} \\ \text{in society} & & \text{by commercial} \\ & & \text{enterprises} \end{array} \quad (1)$$

With

$$\text{Value of goods} \quad = \quad \begin{array}{c} \text{Selling price of} \\ \text{goods at the} \\ \text{commercial} \\ \text{enterprise} \end{array}$$

The difference between the selling price and the purchase price is the income of the commercial enterprise that the production facilities have accepted to cede to commercial enterprises so that commercial enterprises spend on transportation, storage and preservation of goods.

- Then the money from the circulation was collected relying on the **sales** activities of commercial enterprises. Commercial enterprises need to immediately collect money from the buyer right after the sale, so as to ensure no excess money in circulation. By the act of collecting money from the buyer, the money from the circulation is returned to the commercial enterprise.

We always have:

$$\begin{array}{ccc} \text{Total value of} & & \text{Total value of} \\ \text{money is} & & \text{materials, goods} \\ \text{collected from} & = & \text{from commercial} \\ \text{in circulation} & & \text{enterprises are} \\ & & \text{sold} \end{array} \quad (2)$$

And from (1) and (2) we always have:

$$\begin{array}{ccc} & & \text{total value of} \\ \text{Total value of} & & \text{materials, goods} \\ \text{money} & & \text{available} \\ \text{(remaining) in} & = & \text{(remaining) at} \\ \text{circulation} & & \text{commercial} \\ & & \text{enterprises} \end{array} \quad (3)$$

In other words, money in circulation always holds balance with the value of goods in the market (at commercial enterprises).

- Money from the circulation has been collected. After that, if the commercial enterprise buys the goods, the money from the commercial enterprise will be put back into circulation. And then if commercial enterprises sell the goods, the money from the circulation is collected at commercial enterprises.

The process of putting money into circulation and collecting money from circulation goes on and on and on, so it forms a flow of money in society and we always have a balance in value between Goods and Money in the economy always moving and developing, inflation will be eliminated.

Money is put into circulation relied on by commercial enterprises. Accordingly, the source of money for commercial business (buying and selling) does not need to be taken from the income of the society, but simply printed out.

The central bank will print money and provide commercial banks, commercial banks will re-provide according to the needs of commercial enterprises in the form of loans.

Of course, the provision of money to commercial enterprises needs to be managed and controlled in order to avoid abuse, which may have a negative impact on the economy.

2.2.4. Management and control of putting money into circulation

Putting money into circulation by commercial enterprises need to be managed and controlled to prevent commercial enterprises from taking advantage of the money provided or taking advantage of materials and goods purchased for spending or lending indiscriminately, making a part of the money put into circulation without (or losing) materials, goods as evidences, causing disparity (imbalances) in value between Goods and Money in the economy, creating the conditions for inflation to occur. Commercial Banks will manage and control the delivery of money into circulation by commercial enterprises.

We call:

To : The amount of money that commercial enterprise have borrowed from commercial banks to buy and sell goods

T : The amount of money that commercial enterprise has put into and is currently circulating in society

DT   :   The amount of money currently still exists in the funds of commercial enterprise

Q   :   The value of the volume of materials and goods purchased by commercial enterprise and currently remaining in commercial enterprise

(With the value = the sale price in the commercial enterprise itself)

a) If commercial businesses put money into circulation always get materials and goods purchased as evidences to ensure the value for money, if commercial enterprises do not take advantage of the money provided and not take advantage of materials and goods purchased to spend or lend indiscriminately, then we always have:

Total value of materials and goods available at commercial enterprises	>=	Total value of money put into by commercial enterprises and currently circulating in society	(4a)
or Q	>=	T	
Q + DT	>=	T + DT	
Q + DT	>=	To	(4b)

b) If commercial enterprises take advantage of the money provided, or take advantage of materials and goods purchased to spend or lend indiscriminately, causing part of the money being put into circulation does not have materials, goods as evidences to ensure the value for money, then we have:

Total value of materials and goods available at commercial enterprises	<	Total value of money put into by commercial enterprises and currently circulating in society	(5a)
or Q	<	T	
Q + DT	<	T + DT	
Q + DT	<	To	(5b)

Thus, the management and control of commercial businesses put money into circulation can be conducted as follows:

On a regular basis and irregular request, commercial enterprises must prepare the following reports for submission to Commercial Banks:

- Report the value of materials and goods available at
commercial enterprise at the selling prices   Q
(Report of materials and goods in stock at the selling prices)
- Report on the money funds currently existing at commercial
enterprise   DT
- Report on the money that Commercial bank lending to
commercial enterprise to business of buying and selling goods   To

Of course, these reports need to have the actual inspection to ensure the accuracy of data and need to have for specific measures for the cases of dishonesty.

From the above reports:

a) If Q + DT >= To

It proves that the commercial enterprise had put money into circulation and get materials and goods for as control evidences. Commercial businesses do not take advantage of the money provided and also do not take advantage of the amount of materials and goods purchased to spend or lend indiscriminately (Satisfactory).

a) If Q + DT < To

It proves that the commercial enterprise had put money into circulation not had enough materials, goods as control evidences, did not guarantee value of money. Commercial enterprises had taken advantage of the money provided or the amount of materials and goods purchased to spend or lend indiscriminately. Therefore, it is necessary to take specific measures for these commercial enterprises (Unsatisfactory).

Managing and controlling of putting money into circulation by commercial enterprises by the above method is not difficult for us now and can be done absolutely.

As the impact of labor productivity is on the rise, commodity prices are declining, and by the impact of supply and demand rules, commodity prices may rise or fall.

However, throught the management and control as above that money put into circulation will always be regulated with the increase or decrease of commodity prices and we still do not have excessively surplus money in circulation, inflation still does not happen.

Assuming that commercial enterprises have purchased the goods and money have been put into circulation. If then commodity prices rise, the money is put into circulation also increase proportionally (by (4a)) and commercial enterprises benefit. If commodity prices decrease, the money is put into circulation will be reduced to corresponding (by (4a)), the commercial enterprises suffer losses and had to compensate by money income to ensure the (4b) or (4a). Excess money in circulation has not happened, so inflation will not happen.

In short, throught the management and control of the money put into circulation by commercial enterprises as above which the money put into circulation is always balanced against the value of materials and goods on the market. Money put into circulation always get materials, goods as security evidences for value of money, always change corresponding increase or decrease with the increase or decrease in volume of materials, goods on the market, and always change corresponding regulation with the rise and fall of commodity prices on the market (due to the impact of supply-demand and the rule of increasing labor productivity). So inflation will be excluded.

2.2.5. The flow of money in society

The money flow of this alternative can be described as follows:

First, The Central Bank will print money and provide it to commercial banks, Bank of Commerce will use this money to provide it to commercial businesses in the form of loans. Get the money, commercial businesses will buy from anyone who has the goods to sell. From that, the money is put into circulation and began to spread throughout society.

All products produced by the society are to be sold to commercial enterprises, which constitutes the total fund of production, consumption and accumulation of the whole society. Commercial enterprises will reserve and preserve all these products, while the producers who make the products will receive their money by selling their products. When commercial enterprises sell goods, the goods from the reserves are gradually consumed and the money from the circulation is collected.

Getting money from the commercial enterprises after selling goods, it is the source of money for the businesses to payroll for the workers, redistribute income to co-producers, and continue to spend for their process of next re-production.

Getting the money from the results of their labor, it is the source of money for people to spend in whatever field they want to, spending on goods for personal and family use, or investment for manufacturing, basic construction, service business, ... or to spend for their needs of services they want to, such as travel, entertainment, ... to satisfy the current needs and to prepare for their future.

If they spend in the field of procurement of goods, money from circulation is collected, and money is prepared for its next flow, through the relentless buying and selling activities of commercial enterprises in society. If they spend in the service sector, money will continue to circulate in society. And whatever they spend in any field, we always have a balance of value in commodities and money in the ever-moving and developing economy.

Money has come to the members of society. If money is spent in the field of services or other areas (not shopping), money will continue to circulate in society. If money is used to purchase materials and goods, money will be returned to commercial enterprises.

Money is collected at commercial enterprises, it ends its circulation in society and prepares for its next cycle through the continuous buying and selling activities of commercial enterprises.

2.3. BUILDING THE BANKING SYSTEM MODEL FOR MANAGEMENT AND CONTROL OF PUTTING MONEY INTO CIRCULATION UNDER PLAN A

Money put into circulation by commercial enterprises led to the need to build a model of the banking system to manage and control the putting money into circulation by commercial enterprises.

We have the model of the banking system as follows:

We have the model of the Three-level banking system as follows:

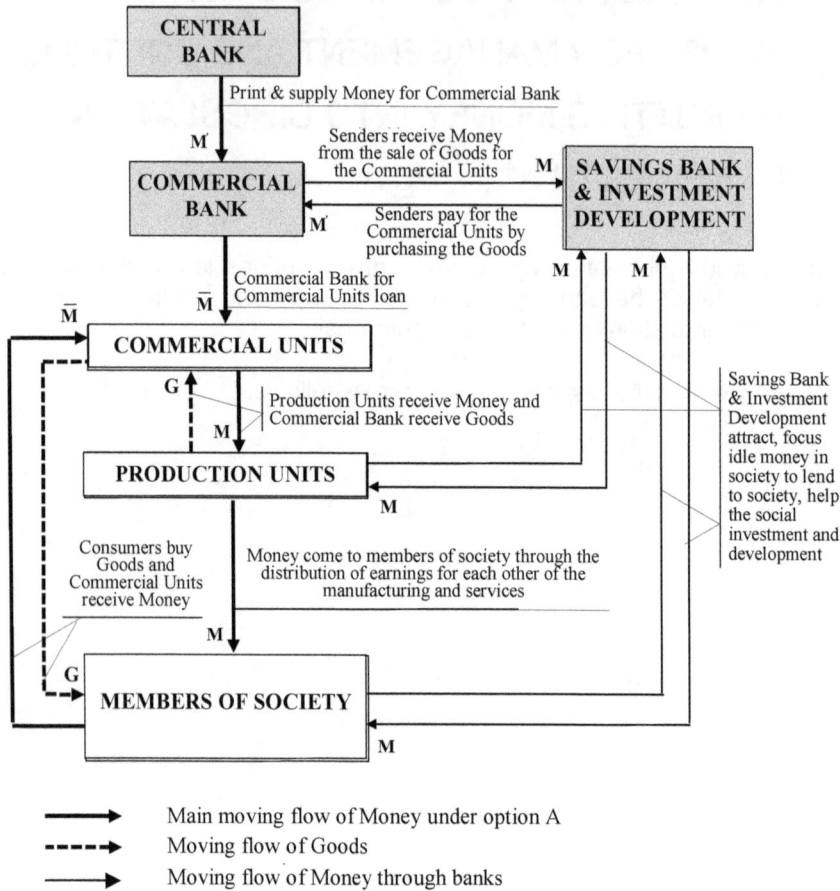

──────▶	Main moving flow of Money under option A
- - - -▶	Moving flow of Goods
──────▶	Moving flow of Money through banks

The banking system built is 3-level banking system:

- Level I: is the central bank, performs the function of issuing money to provide money for the needs of trading activities, exchange, sale and purchase of the economy. The Central Bank monopolized the issuance of money, including bank banknotes, coinage, and book money. The Central Bank does not hand over the issuance of book money to commercial banks, the central bank must monopolize the issuance of money in order to unify control over the total amount of money issued for circulation.

Issuing Principle: The bank issues money not on the basis of gold reserves, but rather through the lending to the economy, on the basis of materials and goods available in the economy. The central bank issues money based on the demand for loans from commercial banks.

The amount of money released, the central bank will supply the economy through the central bank's credit operations to commercial banks. The amount of money obtained is due to issuance, as a result of printing, so the source of money that the Central Bank lending to commercial banks is unlimited loans to meet the fully monetary demand for the operation and development of the economy. The central bank will fully meet the demand for loans from commercial banks. The central bank is only allowed to lend money to commercial banks, not to be allowed to lend money to any other economic institution or individual. The central bank must ensure this principle throughout its operation.

Central Bank has no longer function as the bank of banks in a "lender of last resort " for banks. The central bank only creates solvency for the economy by providing credit to commercial banks, and only the Commercial Bank enjoys this privilege in order to achieve a general balance in terms of value between Goods and Money in the whole economy. Other banks and other credit institutions must create their own ability to pay for themselves. The central bank can not provide credit to these banks and these credit institutions, and so the Central Bank can not provide credit to the Government, can not lend money to the budget, because it must ensure the general balance of value of goods and money in the whole economy.

- Level II: Commercial Banks, which have the functions of sending money (money received from the Central Bank) into circulation in society, through lending money to the commercial enterprises for the purposes of buying and selling goods in the domestic market. Commercial banks are only allowed to lend money to commercial enterprises for buying and selling domestic goods. In addition, commercial banks are not allowed to lend money to any economic organizations nor other individuals, not give any loans for import-export business, not cater for foreign trade.

The source of money that commercial banks have is purely due to borrowings from the central bank's money supply, so commercial banks will lend money to commercial enterprises fully according to the needs of commercial enterprises in order to fully meet the monetary needs for trading, exchanging, buying and selling of the economy.

Loans must be able to repay the loan, and must be used for the right purpose of loan, only used for domestic purchase and sale in the country and not used for any other purposes. The Commercial Bank will manage and control the use of these borrowings by commercial enterprises under Plan A as described above.

- Level III: is the Saving Bank & Investement Development and other credit institutions of the economy.

The Saving Bank & Investement Development and these credit institutions have the function of attracting money that has been put into circulation (by commercial enterprises), concentrating the money of society (temporarily not used) to provide loans for investment in production development, capital construction, service provision, import and export, etc. and other activities of the economy (except for the purpose of domestic trading). The money put into circulation by commercial enterprises so will always balance with the value of materials and goods available on the market, will always have materials and goods available on the market (at Commercial enterprises) as a guarantee of value for money, so the purchasing power of money is always stable, not causing inflation.

The money sources which the Saving Bank & Investement Development gained is due to mobilize from society, not being entitled to credit from the Central Bank as well as commercial banks. Absolutely Central Bank does not provide credit for the Saving Bank & Investement Development. The Saving Bank & Investement Development can obtain money by borrowing from each other or borrowing from foreign banks.

The government, if it wants to make up for the shortfall of the budget, may issue government bonds, term bonds, or borrow money from savings banks and credit institutions. The government does not have the right to print money to spend or borrow money from the Central Bank or the Commercial Bank, as this would break the overall balance of value of Goods and Monies in the economy and so will cause inflation.

* Types of Saving Bank & Investement Development:

Classified in this type of Saving Bank & Investement Development is the following types of banks:

- Agriculture Bank: is a bank dealing in monetary, credit and banking services, mainly in the agricultural sector.

- Industrial Bank is a bank dealing in monetary, credit and banking services, mainly in the fields of industry, transportation, postal services and services (not including trade).

- Bank for Foreign Trade: is a bank dealing in currency, credit and banking services, as a professional foreign trade bank, business scope mainly for export and import, organizing international payments, trading foreign currency and other foreign exchange services.

- Joint-stock bank: is the Bank organized in the form of joint-stock companies, shareholders of bank are composed of many natural persons and legal persons. Shareholders are not allowed to own shares in excess of the ratio stipulated by the State Bank.

- A joint venture bank: is the bank established by capital contributions with a party as the Saving Bank & Investement Development of Vietnam, and a party as a foreign bank.

- Branch of foreign bank: is the establishment of a foreign bank in Vietnam, operating under the law of Vietnam.

- Bank for Investment and Development is a bank dealing in money, credit and banking services, mainly in the field of capital construction.

- Finance Company: is the credit institution dealing in monetary, belongs to the State, or shares.

- Credit cooperative is the credit institution under collective ownership and capital contributed by cooperative members.

Under this 3-level banking system model, the banking system will no longer be able to generate money through the non-cash payment system as it did before. Because the rotation of the money is under control, so it is no longer free to circulate to create a closed system to create money as it did in the previously / currently banking system. The flow of money back to commercial enterprises will be retained, then if there are materials and goods as security objects to ensure value for money, the money will be put back into circulation. If not satisfied the conditions that there are security objects to ensure value for money, the money will not be put back into circulation.

2.4. THE NEW SOLUTION FOR INFLATION STATUS

According to this solution, we will transform the way of putting money into circulation from directly by the government into directly by the   commercial enterprises.

Accordingly, the Government will stop putting money into circulation, and the amount of money (T) that the Government has put into circulation before, because of no control objects to secure the value of money, so will be collected. Then the circulation of money will continue to be made by commercial enterprises. And in order not to cause a major impact on the economy, the volume of money (T) above will be collected and reduced gradually later.

1. First of all, it is necessary to rebuild the functions and tasks of banks in line with the model of the banking system outlined so as to ensure that money is put directly into circulation by commercial enterprises.

2. The Central Bank will print the money and provide it to the Commercial Bank, which the Commercial Bank will provide back to commercial enterprises in the form of a loan, and the commercial enterprises must ensure that the loan is repaid. Then the commercial enterprises will put money into circulation through their buying and selling activities.

3. The Commercial Bank will manage and control the delivery of money into circulation by commercial enterprises.

Constantly and irregularly as required, commercial enterprises shall submit to the Commercial Bank the following reports:

- Report on the value of materials and goods available at commercial enterprises at selling prices   Q
(Report of materials and goods inventory at selling prices)
- Report on the funds currently existing at commercial enterprises   DT
 (Including the types of bank deposits used for the purposes of buying and selling goods)
- Report on the amount of money that commercial enterprises are provided to put into circulation   To

Of course, these reports need to be fact-tested and specific measures must be taken for dishonest cases.

From the above reports:

a) If $Q + DT \geq To$

It proves that commercial enterprises have put money into circulation and had materials and goods as a control evidences to ensure value for money. Commercial enterprises do not take advantage of the money provided and also do not take advantage of the amount of materials and goods purchased to spend or lend indiscriminately (Satisfactory).

It demonstrates that commercial enterprises have used the money provided for the right purpose of buying and selling goods, not used for any other purpose. Commercial enterprises have put money into circulation and had the materials and goods they purchased as control objects for value of money, creating a balance in value between Goods and Money in the economy. Commercial enterprises do not take advantage of the money provided and also do not take advantage of the amount of materials and goods purchased to spend or lend indiscriminately (Satisfactory).

b) If $Q + DT < To$

Demonstrate that commercial enterprises did not use the amount of money provided for the right purpose of buying and selling goods. Commercial enterprises have put money into circulation without enough materials and goods as evidences to ensure value for money. Commercial enterprises have taken advantage of the money provided, or taking advantage of the materials and goods purchased to spend or lend indiscriminately, causing a portion of the money put into circulation without (or loss) materials, goods as control objects for value of money, causing imbalances in value between goods and money in the economy, creating conditions for inflation recur. Therefore, measures need to be taken against these commercial enterprises (Unsatisfactory).

To avoid using the money for improper purposes, first commercial bank lend money to commercial enterprises, with interest rate currently available on the market. Then, if the commercial enterprises meet the requirements stated above, they will be rewarded with 70-90% interest rate. If the commercial enterprises fail to meet these requirements, they will not be awarded interest rates but also be subject to warning or no longer have the right to borrow money from commercial banks because they have violated the principle of putting money into circulation and threatens the sustainability of the overall balance of value of goods and money across the economy.

4. Along with putting the money into circulation as above, the Ministry of Finance will collect the amount of money (T) that the Government previously put into circulation (but can not have any objects as evidence to ensure value for money) to eliminate the natural cause of inflation, contributing to the stability of the economy.

The amount of money (T) above is collected by offsetting from the budget or a volume of public property that is sold. This process will be carried out over a relatively long period of time so as not to cause major fluctuations in the economy (5 years, 10 years, ...).

The volume of money (T) obtained, the Ministry of Finance will pay back to the Central Bank, and the money will then be put into circulation by commercial enterprises under plan A as above. The amount of money (T) is fully collected will eliminate the natural cause of inflation, contributing to the stability of the economy. The volume of money (T) is fully collected, the balance relationship in terms of value between goods and currency will be established, inflation will be excluded.

*
* *

However, it is still possible that the government does not have the ability to recover the amount of money (T), because the budget is too tight and the government does not have the assets to sell, then the society still needs to be put more money into circulation to meet the need for more money for the operation and development of the economy. In this case, we will still put money more into circulation relying on commercial enterprises in accordance with the plan A above to continuously meet the monetary needs for the development of the economy, and will gradually eliminate inflation.

Money is still added to the circulation by commercial enterprises as above. Inflation is still occurring, commodity prices are still rising, due to the volume of money (T) without any evidences to ensure its value, was not collected. Money is constantly being added to circulation to meet the need for more money in the flow of the economy.

Money is constantly being added to circulation by the commercial enterprises as above until the volume of money (T) is smaller than the total amount of money added to circulation, the price will gradually go into stability, the influence of inflation will gradually decrease over time.

Money is still constantly added to circulation as above to continually respond to the need for more money circulating in the economy. As long as the volume of money (T) is many times smaller than the total amount of money added to circulation, then the value relationship between the Goods and the Money can now be almost reached at equilibrium, inflation is still occurring, commodity prices are still rising but at a smaller scale, getting smaller and smaller, and we can actually see inflation as excluded.

And money is constantly being added to the circulation by commercial enterprises under plan A as above to continuously meet the need for money for the operation and development of the economy. Over time, the effects of inflation on the economy and for all of us will be no longer. Money will be used as an intermediary to facilitate the exchange of products of people in society in an easy, quick and convenient manner, helping for the operation and development of the economy, and it is no longer the cause of the disorder in the economy, no longer cause inflation.

CHAPTER 3

CONCLUSION

The method of putting money into circulation by commercial enterprises under plan A creates a fully automatic mechanism, always adjusting the volume of money in circulation increase or decrease corresponding to the fluctuation up or down of the economy, so there would be no need for any intervention by the Government or the Central Bank in regulating the increase or reduction of the circulation of money in society.

The way of putting money into circulation by the commercial enterprises under plan A always create a relationship between money and market being real nice and homogeneous, it eliminates the redundancy of money as well as the lack of money in circulation, therefore, the situation of weak purchasing power of the people can not buy the goods will be no longer. The situation is only due to lack of money in circulation.

For now, all the products produced by people are sold to commercial enterprises and they will receive money immediately, provided that the product is able to be exchanged and sold in the market. People receive immediate money from selling their products, which will increase the aggregate demand in the economy, stimulating the purchasing power of the whole society.

Money put into circulation by commercial enterprises, the source of money for the Government and the commercial enterprises trade in buying and selling of goods is unlimited; And money put into circulation by commercial enterprises, through which the Government controls commercial enterprises.

Therefore, the Government will grasp important sources of goods, control the market, prevent speculation and raise prices causing market disturbances. From there, in the market, between supply and demand will be met in harmony, materials and goods will have appropriate reserves, between production and consumption will find a common voice compatible, avoid the scarcity as well as redundancy of goods.

Money put into circulation by commercial enterprises, which will help the commercial sector to have a virtually unlimited working capital to trade in the buying and selling of goods. This will help to create a commercial network system throughout the country, creating a boom for the commercial sector. The Vietnam-commerce enterprises will grow constantly and will not be inferior to the world's leading trading companies being and will invest in Vietnam.

Money put into circulation by the commercial enterprises under plan A, so money always has materials, goods as a guarantee of value of money, and gold will no longer play the role of determining the value of money as before. Gold is just a normal commodity like other commodities in society, and the value of money is due to the stability of the balance relationships in value between commodities and money decide. It depends on whether money put into circulation obtain materials, goods as security for value or not.

Countries in the world have not successfully eliminated inflation, even advanced countries such as Britain, France, USA, Russia, China, ... all the same. They have to accept suffered a loss equivalent to 4% of gross national product to reduce inflation by 1%, but inflation is recurring many times without being able to eliminate it. And now we do not need such expensive anymore. We just need to create a balance between the value of Goods and Money in the economy, and the way of putting money into circulation by commercial enterprises under the project A is implemented, inflation will be eliminated.

Always create a balance of value between Goods and Money in the economy always moving and developing, this solution will help the Government of Vietnam as well as other countries around the world is no longer to cause inflation anymore. The value of the national currency is built on the basis of the true internal force of the economy; it does not depend on the psychological fluctuations as well as on the beliefs of the people in society, and everyone will automatically acknowledge and trust their national currency. The value of the national currency will always be maintained, stable, and will have a solid value no worse than any other currency in the world.

Establishing a balance of value between commodities and money and always keeping that balance in the always-moving and developing economy, so the value of the national currency will always be stable, contributing to prevent currency crises. Everyone in every country can be proud of their country's currency as proud of their nation's flag.

Establishing a balance of value between commodities and money and always maintaining that balance in a constantly moving and developing economy, which will help countries gradually come to unification with the common use of a single currency in the world. Countries will exchange goods and services for each other easily, quickly and conveniently in a globalized world.

By putting money into circulation directly through commercial enterprises, we will no longer worry about inflation or recession, no longer worrying about excess or lack of money in circulation, government and The central bank no longer has to worry about withdrawing money or putting money into circulation, no longer having to worry about raising interest rates or lowering interest rates, drawing money from circulation or putting more money into circulation to fight inflation or stimulate demand against economic recession, ...

Money put into circulation by commercial enterprises always creates a balance of value between commodities and money in the economy always moving and developing, the rotation of the money will no longer be dependent on the psychology of consumers, the lack of money in circulation will not occur. The balance of values between Goods and Money will always be established, in which society will always have the money to buy the goods that society produces. The accumulation of goods, stagnation of production, economic recession will not occur. The cyclical cycle of growth and degradation, inflation and recession will no longer occur, and the economy will develop stably and sustainably.

Written by NGUYEN CAO DUNG

APPENDIX

THE FEASIBILITY OF THE SOLUTION - THE FEASIBILITY OF 3-LEVEL BANKING SYSTEM MODEL

The feasibility of this solution - a new solution to inflation - largely depends on the feasibility of developing and implementing a three-level banking system. Therefore, to study the feasibility of the solution, we just need to focus on the feasibility of the three-level banking system.

Building a three-level banking system is not difficult for us today, it is in our power. We will still maintain the status quo of the currently existing Commercial Bank (old) but its name is reset to Saving Bank & Investement Development and its functions have also changed; simultaneously build new commercial banks with new functions.

Central Bank, the activities of the Central Bank remain the same, has not changed much, it just changes in lending money to other banks, and the central bank has no longer function as Bank of banks in the role as "lender of last resort" for banks. The Central Bank only lends money to commercial banks. The central bank is not allowed to grant credit to any bank, credit institution, individual or other organization, including without advance payment for government budgets.

Bank of Commerce (New), Saving Bank & Investement Development - The reality of these two banks is just the separation of the former commercial banks into two types of new banks, with different functions, in order to carry out a specialization one step further in banking operations, it does not cause difficulties, obstacles to the operation of the bank.

The Commercial Bank (new) only serves commercial enterprises, only serves payment for purchases and sales in Vietnamese Dong to commercial enterprises, and the Saving Bank & Investement Development serves the remaining subjects of the economy.

The new Commercial Bank will provide credit to commercial enterprises and thereby bring money into circulation through the buying and selling activities of commercial enterprises. The Saving Bank & Investement Development will attract the amount of money that has been put into circulation in the society (from commercial enterprises) to concentrate production loans and develop the economy.

Commercial Bank (new) is an organization serving only to objects related to commercial activities (buying and selling of goods), only for the domestic trading activities of commercial enterprises, not to serve other objects, not cater to foreign trade, import-export and other purposes.

Saving Bank & Investement Development is an organization that caters to the objects of production, capital construction, foreign trade, import and export and other types of services and other activities of the economy, except only for domestic trade. The Saving Bank & Investement Development will take part of the world economic integration, economic and financial affairs related to foreign trade, import-export business, foreign exchange services, organized of international payment, trading foreign currency, ...

The source of capital for Commercial Bank (New) operating, is due to credit entirely from the source of money issued by the Central Bank, in addition, should not get money from any other source, no need to mobilize from the savings in society.

The source of capital for Saving Bank & Investement Development operating, is due to mobilize from the source of savings, from the money currently temporarily idle in the society.

The Saving Bank & Investement Development does not serve the commercial sector to accrue capital for production and development investment. Anyone who wants to be serviced in commercial sector, there will be Commercial Bank (new), the Commercial Bank (new) will be able to provide a full loan on demand as long as the loan is used properly for the right purpose of buying and selling goods in domestic market, not used for any other purpose, and must make sure to repay the loan.

The separation of the currently old Commercial Bank into two levels of the new bank is only a specialization one step further in banking operations, it is not difficult for us today.

Building a three-level banking system, the separation of the old Commercial Bank into two new levels of the new bank, is completely within our current capacity, and furthermore we will always have a balance of value between Goods and Money in the economy, inflation will be eliminated. We will get out of the spiral: money supply - inflation - recession. The value of the national currency will always be firm and stable. The economy will develop quickly, stably and sustainably.

According to Paul A. Samuelson & William D. Norhaus, to reduce inflation by one percent, they must accept a loss equivalent to 4 percent of the gross national product. This solution - a new solution to the problem of inflation - will help the economy no longer have such a great expensive to solve the inflation problem.

The core problem of inflation is not due to the trade deficit or the domestic production capacity is too weak. Even though national production capacity is weak or strong, productivity is low or high, manufactured goods are more or less, quality of goods is good or not good as expected, imports are more or less..., only when there are the goods as control evidences to ensure the value of money, at that time the money will be put into circulation, and when the goods have been sold for consumption, money from the circulation will be collected, so it will not cause inflation.

The government and the central bank / central bank will control putting money into circulation always correspond to the value of the volume of goods available in the economy, and especially not to print money for consumption or lend to spend, it will not cause inflation.

This solution is simple and effective, not complicated, just redistribute functions, and specialize the activities of current commercial banks will be successful.

This solution will be of great help to the Government. The administration of monetary policy by the Government and the State Bank / Central Bank will be much more gentle and effective. The government will no longer have to worry about whether to fight inflation or economic recession. The government will no longer have to worry about excess or lack of money in circulation, raise interest rates or lower interest rates, absorb money from circulation to fight inflation or put more money into circulation to stimulate demand for anti-economic recession, ... Cyclical spiral: growth and recession, inflation and recession will no longer occur, the economy will develop rapidly, stable and sustainable.

PAUL SAMUELSON'S INFLATION CONTROL MEASURES ARE JUST THE SITUATIONAL MEASURES

In the control of inflation, Paul Samuelson's macroeconomic regulation can only be applied to Vietnam (as well as other countries in the world) in a situational measure to curb inflation, it can not be a radical, long-term solution to the problem of inflation. The reason is because the measure putting money in circulation of Paul Samuelson still based on two-level bank system, still putting money into circulation primarily by printing money for consumption or lending to spend, so sooner or later it happens inflation. The more the money put into circulation, the higher the inflation.

Adopting Paul Samuelson's macroeconomics, the tightening of the monetary will solve the situation, curbing inflation at this time, but there is a shortage of liquidity shortly thereafter. Then again loosening monetary needs for the development of the economy, then continue to occur inflation, then tighten the monetary, ... And then go on such a vicious circle, inflation has repeatedly re-recurring so many times, inflation continues to go along with the development of the economy and still can not cure definitive inflation. Paul Samuelson just solved the tops (symptoms) of inflation, but did not solve the root (cause) of inflation.

Thus, Paul Samuelson's inflation control measures are only a temporary measure, not a long-term strategy to tackle inflation.

CAUSES AND SOLUTIONS TO INFLATION TO SAVE THE MARKET ECONOMY

The cause of inflation in recent years is because of the consequence of previous years caused:

1. Mainly due to previous years, the government (in Vietnam as well as in other countries) printed money to cover the shortfall of the budget, and / or due to the Government printed money to other economic organizations for loans to invest in production, capital construction ... but the government did not have any related evidences to ensure value for money. Society sells his goods to the government and collects money but the society does not have other goods to buy, because the government does not have any corresponding reference goods to secure the value of money, thus creating pressure that causes the imbalance in value of goods and money in the economy, causing inflation.

That is the cause of all causes of inflation as before and today. Other causes such as cost inflation, demand pull inflation, psychological inflation ... are all caused by that.

2. Inflation in Vietnam as in other countries is also due to a type of mechanism as above, but inflation in different countries has different in levels, scales and time of inflation. At this time there are countries with high levels of inflation, other countries have low inflation. Countries have different currencies, trading goods and services together through exchange rates. Thus inflation in this country may be transferred to another country through this exchange rate regime. The rise in prices in this country may also cause prices to rise in other countries and vice versa. We now call it import (or export) inflation. This country imports goods from country with inflation (commodity prices rise), it also imports inflation, while other country exports inflation.

3. The deeper root cause of inflation, in my opinion, may be that the government (as well as the people) does not have a full understanding of the monetary (which is essentially paper money), so they did not know how to release and use the monetary properly, reasonably and more scientifically so as not to cause inflation. You can see more 1.1. Paper money is only a special type of coupon to better understand.

On the solution of inflation to save the market economy that other countries as well as Vietnam should implement:

Monetary policy of the State Bank / Central Bank is the key to growth and inflation. In my opinion, the key point is: If the State Bank has monetary policy, credit growth (from the money issued) is only to develop trade (buying and selling goods only), thereby developing the economy, will not cause Inflation, and will escape the spiral cycle: money supply - inflation - recession.

Of course, do not print out money to spend or lend to spend.

The credit growth (from the money issued) through the commercial enterprises borrowing money (from the money issued) to make purchases and sales of goods, always have the goods purchased as a related evidences to ensure the value for money, always create and ensure the balance of value between goods and money in the economy, having money is that having goods to buy, so it does not cause inflation. The State Bank will address two issues: both to increase credit to meet the demand for economic growth and still not to cause inflation, and thus the inflation problem has been solved. The economy will grow as fast as it can and inflation will no longer happen.

Please see further Section 2.4. The new solution for inflation status to understand better.

THE COUPON IS THE ORIGINAL FORM OF THE BANKNOTE

In the process of forming and developing the paper money, in the beginning, gold, silver was replaced by gold certificates, silver certificates issued by banks received deposit of gold, silver, and it is given to those who have deposited gold, silver. By using these receipts / certificates, the person who owns it can buy the other products, goods he needs.

When want to receive back gold, silver, those depositors will return the receipts / certificates to the bank, and the bank will return gold and silver to them according to the amount of gold and silver recorded on the receipt / certificate, then the receipt / certificate will be destroyed.

Thus, these receipts/ certificates was valid and used as a coupon of gold, silver, and issued by the bank. These receipts / certificates are identical to the coupon, are a different form of coupon more expanded, with more details and are issued by the bank. After the depositors receives back the gold and silver, the coupons are returned and destroyed.

Over time, in order to facilitate easy the payment of the amount of gold and silver deposited, those coupons, those receipts / certificates of gold and silver, have been simplified, simplified and improved.

It no longer record the name, ID number, address, ... of the gold and silver depositors. It no longer specifies the amount of gold and silver that is deposited, instead it is standardized by writing the value numbers. It is capable of exchanging gold and silver freely at the issuing banks, with gold and silver volumes corresponding to the value figures written on it. The process of simplification and improvement has been going on for a long time, and since then it has become like today's paper money.

And those kinds of coupon, those receipts / certificates of gold and silver deposits issued by banks before, were considered as early forms of paper money.

More broadly, the types of coupons used in the previously planned and subsidized economy, these types of coupons have been improved and unified into a special type of coupon: paper money. Therefore, these types of coupons can absolutely be considered as the original forms of paper money.

In summary, coupons also exist in other forms, such as receipts / certificates of gold and silver deposits. A coupon is an early form of paper money, which is present earlier than paper money, but it is not, is not yet paper money. After a simplified process that improves both the external appearance and the intrinsic content of the inner values, having the concept of inside value, then it becomes the paper money.

WHY PAPER MONEY DOES NOT NEED REAL VALUE

In the process of circulation and exchange of goods, at first, the currency appeared in the form of gold bullion, silver ingots. In the process of circulation and exchange, the gold and silver money is gradually wearing out and losing some of its value, but it is still accepted by society as gold, silver and silver with full value. Thus, the real value of money is separate from its nominal value. The reason for this situation is that money (as a medium of exchange) only plays a role for a moment, people exchange goods for money and then use the money to buy the goods that they need.

As a means of exchange, money does not necessarily have full value. Taking advantage of that situation, when minting money, the state seeks to reduce the metal content of the monetary units. The real value of coinage is lower and lower than its nominal value. From that practice led to the birth of paper money. Money itself is not valuable, but only a sign of value, and recognized within the country. In the 18th century, European countries attempted to issue paper money to eliminate the financial difficulties of the state.

However, when the government was in debt due to the wars that had arisen, plus the mass issuance of large amounts of paper money to offset the financial balance, which was make this paper money lose its value. Putting too much paper money into circulation has caused inflation, which is very harmful to the economy of a country. Due to these problems, gradually people lose faith in paper money, no longer prefer to use it anymore.

The real value of the banknote is much lower than the nominal value that it represents, its use value specified in the law is the medium of exchange, people use paper money based on credibility with the central bank. Total amount of money in circulation reflects the division of national product: The amount of money a person owns / possesses corresponds to the amount of national product that he or she may have, when he or she consumes his or her amount of money. Monetary developments, from the era of metal coins until the time of paper money removed metal coins, was a new development of quality, and has opened the beginning of a new era.

STORAGE FUNCTION OF PAPER MONEY

As you know, the purpose of putting money (paper money) into circulation in society is to make money as an intermediary to facilitate the exchange of goods of people for each other is easy, fast and convenient through the activities of buying and selling goods in the market, thereby helping the operation, growth and development of the economy. Here you should also note that the growth and development economy is the consequence (not the purpose) of putting money into circulation.

Using money (paper money) as an intermediary to facilitate the exchange of goods, people will first bring the goods (or services) that they have, **to sell** in exchange for money. Then people will use the money that they have just earned **to buy** other goods (or services) that they need. These two processes of sales and purchase take place sequentially seperately, separated by a certain period of time. The length of time between the sale and purchase is the length of the storage and circulation of paper money. People store paper money, which also means people temporarily do not yet want to use paper money in exchange for goods (or services) they do not really yet need.

Paper money is a special type of coupon, a special type of debt paper of society (such as commercial enterprises) for those who own it.

People store paper money, which is also an indirect way to store their goods, possessions, assets temporarily unused; And these goods, possessions, assets are stored and safe-kept temporary by commercial enterprises for those who own or hold paper money.

In the short term, paper money is always capable of carrying out storage functions if people still have faith and trust in its (purchasing power) value.

In the long term, if paper money is abused, issued paper money to spend or lend to spend, which will lead to inflation, rising commodity prices, the purchasing power of paper money will be chipped and reduced down. Because the purchasing power of paper money is reduced, people will no longer want to keep their paper money in the long term, but they will convert their paper money into other assets of more sustainable value over time as gold, silver, real estate, ...

In short, both in the short and long term, if paper money is issued and put into circulation for the sole purpose of making paper money as an intermediary for exchange, to facilitate the exchange of goods of people for each other in society, do not abuse the issuance of paper money to spend or lend to spend, the paper money will always have the ability to perform storing function in a stable manner, long-term and sustainable, people's money pocket will not be reduced purchasing power over time.

THE DIFFERENCE BETWEEN PAPER MONEY AND OTHER TYPES OF MONEY

From very early in human history there has appeared a essential need for a form of monetary as an intermediary for product exchange. Aboriginal people on the coast of Asia and Africa, formerly used shells, seashells as monetary. Wheat and barley are used in Mesopotamia, rice is used in the Philippines archipelago. In China, millet seeds and silk are used as money.

Using commodities for as money as above has some inconveniences during the exchange process, such as perishable, inhomogeneous ... so it is not accepted by everyone everywhere, thus leading to the use of metal coins. Gradually, people have agreed to use precious metals such as gold and silver to fabricate into money. But the amount of precious metals, such as gold and silver, is not much in comparison to the increasing demand for commodity exchange in society, which has led to the birth and development of paper money.

At first, the paper money is insured in gold, silver. The value of paper money is derived from the value of the reciprocal material (such as gold, silver,... deposited at the bank) on which the paper money represents them. Paper money is described as the most advanced money. However, because governments have abused, released and put too much paper money into circulation, it has caused inflation. Due to these problems, people gradually lose faith in it, no longer prefer to use paper money.

So today, in order to ensure the value of paper money, the value of the paper money must be formed and secured by the value of the reciprocal objects, by the value of the materials and goods (including gold, silver, ...) available in the market (at commercial enterprises).

Coins in gold, silver is a special commodity, which itself guarantees its value. Gold, silver itself can buy itself, so the release of coins in gold, silver much more and more still does not cause inflation.

Paper money is a special type of coupon, a special type of debt paper of society (such as commercial businesses) for those who own it. Whoever has paper money, that person may request society (such as commercial businesses) bring back (return) by the specific commodities with the value corresponding to the value recorded on the paper money. The paper money has no intrinsic value, itself can not guarantee its own value, so the issuance of too much paper money that there is no basis, no objects to ensure value for money, will cause inflation.

The difference between paper money and money of gold, silver can be summarized as follows:

- The difference in time of formation: Money of gold, silver appeared before, paper money appeared after.

- The difference in constituent materials: Money of gold, silver is made of gold, silver, and paper money is made primarily of paper material.

- The difference in nature: Money of gold, silver is a kind of special goods, and paper money is a kind of special coupon, special type of debt paper.

- The difference in the objects ensuring the value of money: To money of gold, silver, objects ensuring the value of money of gold, silver lie inside itself of gold, silver making up currency. While, to paper money, objects ensuring the value of paper money lie outside of the currency.

- The difference in the results of release: issuing coins of gold, silver how much more also still not cause inflation, and issuing banknotes abused too much, will cause inflation.

Over here we have talked about the difference between money of gold, silver and paper money. Other forms such as book money, electronic money, checks, ... are also considered other forms of money to replace banknotes / coins of gold, silver. It is also considered as the payment instrument to help for the transfer and the payment of money, settle debts expressed in money for each other to be safe, fast, and convenient.

TO DEAL WITH INFLATION, WHAT CONSUMERS SHOULD DO TO REDUCE INFLATION

Consumers are always the victims of inflation unless they are rich and / or do not care about the rise in commodity prices.

To deal with inflation, with the desire to reduce inflation, prevent the recurrence of repeated recurrence of inflation, consumers can through the Consumer Protection Association to impact on subjects who cause inflation:

- Call on / Recommend to the Government (in countries around the world) try not to print money to spend or to lend to spend anymore in order to not cause inflation so as not to harm the money pocket of the consumer anymore. After all, these money are not due to the labor of Government created, so the Government should not use it to spend, and also should not lend it to other organizations to spend.

Moreover, the printing of money to spend or to lend to spend always contains the risk of inflation, sooner or later inflation also occurs, causing the inhibition and harm to consumers as well as the development of the economy. The printing of money to spend or to lend to spend thus can not take advantage of and mobilize all potential of the whole society to accelerate the pace of economic development and improve people's quality of life.

- Call on/ Recommend to the Government (in countries around the world) attach importance to, prioritize trade development, cares and takes care of the output for all types of products and goods that economy produces, control the rotation of the money, stabilize the market prices. The source of capital (working capital) for commercial development will be taken from the source of money released by the State Bank / Central Bank.

The development of the trade sector will lead to the development of the whole economy, thereby increasing the revenues of the government budget without causing inflation and / or economic recession.

The source of money, after being put into circulation from commercial enterprises, will be the source of money for investment in capital construction, production development, budgeting, and consumption for organizations and individuals,... This source of money, because there is always the guarantee of balance between the value of goods and money in the market (at commercial enterprises), so does not cause inflation, not to harm the money pocket of consumers in the society.

In the solving of the inflation problem, the application of the balance of values between Goods and Money is just the necessary condition, and **the sufficient condition** to not cause inflation is Do Not print money to spend or to lend to spend. Having done so, we can completely solve the problem of inflation, recession, and prevent the economic crisis.

- Consumers should also positively deposit money into the bank, purchase government bonds, term bonds to contribute to limiting inflation.

POSITIVELY DEPOSITING SAVINGS INTO BANKS CONTRIBUTES TO LIMITING INFLATION

1. Actively depositing money into banks contributes to increasing the circulation of money, both useful for the country, both for the benefit of the family:

Savings Bank is a credit intermediary organizations that is both a borrower and a lender, borrowing to lend. By depositing savings into banks, the depositors will receive deposit rates, and at the same time it will help the bank raise additional funds to lend to other organizations and individuals for consumption or production development, service, ... Thereby increasing the speed of rotation of money, it also means that increasing the speed of consumption of goods, stimulate production as well as the whole economy to grow. So actively depositing your savings into banks will be helpful for yourself, for others, for your society as well as for the growth of the entire economy.

2. Citizens should not keep much cash but should actively deposit savings into banks to contribute to limiting inflation:

So far, inflation is still a constant threat to the development of the economies of countries around the world. In countries around the world, money (paper money) is put into circulation, money is freely circulated in the society but the flow of money is not controlled, so inflation is not just due to the release too lots of money into circulation but also depends on the speed of circulation / rotation of money. The speed of circulation / rotation of money depends on the psychology of the people.

In times of high inflation, people's psychology is very unstable. The psychology of the people, the belief of the people in the value of the money is reduced, the speed of circulation / rotation of the money increased, amplified which made inflation rise rapidly. Because the commodity prices go up continuously, the devaluation of money go down constantly, people no longer have faith in the value of money, no longer want to keep cash in hand or bank, but just want to turn it into goods (or gold, foreign currency, real estate, etc.) with the desire to reduce losses and to self-protect for their life source and their own economic benefit.

The speed of circulation / rotation of the currency due to the psychology of people (fear of the devaluation of money) amplifies the speed up very quickly, making goods increasingly scarce, the more do for galloping inflation goes up very fast. Inflation is now rising rapidly due to the psychology of the people, in which the point of the original onset is due to previously paper money was released and put too much into circulation caused.

In times of inflation, banks have to raise interest rates (interest rates need to be higher than inflation rates) to attract money into banks, keep money back at banks, slow down the pace of circulation of money, stabilize the psychology of the people, reduce the pressure of the money on the goods, thereby curb, limit the increase in commodity prices, restrict inflation.

Therefore, citizens should not keep much cash but should actively deposit savings into banks to contribute to limiting inflation.

3. Savings deposited in the bank (or buy government bonds, term bonds) will then be used to spend, invest, but may not be as effective as expected, the investment project may fail, inefficient. Having this project succeeded, another project failed. But it is important that there are the sources of bank deposits (or the source of money that has bought government bonds, term bonds) of the people, so the government and society have capital sources to invest. As a result, the government will not need to print money to invest or lend to invest, and therefore (not print money to invest, spend) will not cause inflation.

Depositing savings into banks (or buying government bonds, term bonds) of people is therefore always significant in contributing to restrict inflation.

INCREASE SALARY MAY LEAD TO INCREASE INFLATION ?

The increase in the basic wage or salary increase in general, itself does not say whether it will increase inflation or not. It is important that where the source of the money to raise salary will be taken from.

As you saw in the article analyzing Why there is inflation, the article have demonstrated and the conclusion is: If we (the whole society) live and spend on our own incomes, we (the whole society) will always have enough goods to buy and the prices of goods will not be increased.

In the article To deal with inflation, what consumers should do to reduce inflation, which has written as "**The sufficient condition** to not cause inflation is Do Not print money to spend or to lend to spend". This sentence is also inferred from the analysis of Why there is inflation is mentioned above.

So, if the source of the money to increase wages is taken from the income of the whole society (including from the budget's tax revenues, or from the reduction of a part of the profits of the businesses or bank loans from the savings of society, ...) will not cause inflation. If the source of money to raise wages is taken from the source of money issued or borrowed from the money issued (printed money to spend or to lend to spend), it will cause inflation.

Currently inflation is rising. In order to ensure the livelihood of workers, it is necessary to compensate for the increase in the price of the goods, and the wages of the workers must be increased in proportion to the rate of inflation. If the wage increase is derived from the income of the society, which will not cause inflation.

At present, in society, prices are rising, so we feel that the source of money to increase wages will contribute to increasing inflation. In fact, prices are still rising as consequences of past years caused, and the source of money to rise the new wages (derived from social income) will not contribute to inflation up.

P/s- You can refer to or rely on the answers above to expand and answer questions such as increased budgetary spending, budget overspending, increased spending on investment in production development, increasing expenditures on capital construction, public works, infrastructure of industrial zones, export processing zones to attract foreign investment, etc., will cause inflation or not.

THE CURRENCY OF ANY COUNTRY CAN BECOME A STRONG FOREIGN CURRENCY

The problem of a country's inflation does not need to depend on whether the country has a lot of gold, silver, mineral resources or not. Such as Singapore, Japan, ... just a small country with few mineral resources but a wealthy country, they rarely have budget deficits. Their government has no / rarely thought of printing money to offset the budget deficit. Just do not print money to spend, only that alone has also helped them to limit and greatly reduce the impact of inflation on the economy of their country.

The currency of any country, whether the country is small or large, may well become a strong currency, provided that the currency of that country printed and put into circulation just only for the sole purpose is for MONEY functioning as a means of exchange, to facilitate the exchange of purchase and sale of goods, and not to take advantage of the use of money issued for any other purpose.

Money should only be released and put into the circulation through channels for commercial businesses borrowing money to perform the function of exchanging goods, help for the purchase, sale and exchange of goods of people for each other in society.

It is not allowed to take advantage of the direct use of the source of money released for the development of production, investment in the construction of technical infrastructure, public works, etc... But it is necessary to use indirectly the source of money released (after being put into circulation by commercial enterprises) to develop production, make up for budget, invest in technical infrastructure, public works ... to always ensure the balance of value between Goods and Money in the economy, maintain and stabilize the value for money.

Just adhere to the simple manner like that is going to succeed. The value of national currency will be maintained, stable, and will become strong currency (strong foreign currency) with solid value, and not inferior to any other currency in the world. Not necessarily the currency of a big country with many mineral resources, it can well become the strong currency (strong foreign currencies).

THE SOURCE OF MONEY FOR INVESTMENT, SPENDING AND CIRCULATION OF MONEY IN SOCIETY

In order to eradicate inflation, the source of money for investment and consumption needs to be derived from the income of the society, from the proceeds of the sale of goods (or services) to the Commercial enterprises and society. This proceeds will then be distributed by businesses to everyone in society through paying taxes on the budget, paying employees, re-distributing income for co-producers of goods, and continued spending on the process of re-production and investment.

It is forbidden to directly use the source of money issued to invest, spend (or lend to invest and spend) so as not to cause a imbalance in the value of goods and money in the economy. So as not to cause inflation, not to harm the monetary pockets of consumers in society.

The money released should only be put in / pump into circulation through the channel for commercial enterprises borrowing, so that money can help people buy, sell and exchange goods for each other in society, not to cause inflation. With money borrowed from the source of money released, commercial enterprises will buy the goods and pay immediately to anyone who has the goods to sell them, as long as the goods are likely to sell, consume on the market. Since then the money was put into circulation and began to spread throughout society. This money always corresponds to the value of materials and goods purchased by commercial enterprises, so it does not cause inflation.

After selling goods to commercial enterprises and collecting the money right away, it is the source of money for production enterprises to spend on their next re-production, investment in product development, pay taxes to the budget, pay salaries to employees, and distribute income to those who work together to create those products.

If used in the field of services with products of spiritual value such as culture, education, health, entertainment, tourism, ... or other service areas such as payment for electricity, phone, internet, transportation, insurance, etc., money will continue to be circulated in the society, and that money will be redistributed to members of businesses in the field of service business.

Money from commercial enterprises reaches the members of society, the whole society (businesses, government budgets, workers' organizations and individuals ...) will have a legitimate source of income from their own labor to spend on organizations, individuals and families, spending on the need for re-production, spending on production development, capital construction, development of technical infrastructure, construction of public works, ...

If used to purchase materials and goods for investment or consumption, money will be returned to commercial enterprises. Money is returned and collected at commercial enterprises, it ends its cycle in society and prepares for the next cycle due to the constant activities of buying and selling goods of commercial enterprises in society. Then, as businesses continue to sell goods to commercial enterprises, money from commercial enterprises will be brought back into circulation, the society will continue to have the money to invest, spend. And the circulation of money continuously goes on in such a process in society.

OUTPUT PRODUCTS FOR FARM ECONOMY

To encourage the farm economy, I think the Government should have a price and consumption policy to buy, support and resolve output for farm economy. Accordingly, the government should build a commercial network throughout the rural areas in order to be ready to buy and consume all kinds of agricultural products produced by farmers, making sure farmers are profitable and have a stable source of income.

This is also an effective stimulus method for the rural market, creating a legitimate source of income for farmers. The capital [working capital] that commercial establishments achieved are the borrowing from the "source of money issued" by the State Bank. This commercial network is to help the consumption of products made by the people so it needs to have the consent, support and participation of people In solving their own life problems.

Rural is a large market that accounts for 80% of the country's population, but this potential has not been fully exploited. When there is output for the products, and a source of income guaranteed, farmers will buy each other's farm goods and buy other things they need. They just need to buy each other's farm products, that also helps them consume a large proportion of the farm products that they produced. Thus the direction to solve a large part of the output for the agricultural economy in general, including farms, has been opened. They also have other markets such as the urban market of industrial producers, services and export markets.

[Commercial establishments] Buy all the products produced by the people [From the source of money issued], through which the Government will control the market, grasp the supply and demand situation for each kind of goods. From that can help manufacturers to come up with suitable production options, avoid waste. Between production and consumption will find a common voice compatible, avoid overproduction as well as shortage of goods. Simultaneously, try not to reduce the purchase price of agricultural products of farmers lower than the floor price specified for each type of agricultural products.

We use the power of the peasants to solve their own problems, which require government assistance in terms of purchasing policies, consumption, and an appropriate pricing strategy, if the commercial establishments suffer losses, they will be compensated by the financial reserve fund and the price stabilization fund.

Written by NGUYEN CAO DUNG

Copyright reserved. Please quote the source and author's name.

REFERENCES

1 - Economics, Volume 1 - PAUL A. SAMUELSON, WILLIAM D. NORDHAUS - Institute for International Relations, 1989, Vietnam.

2- Economics, Volume 2 - PAUL A. SAMUELSON, WILLIAM D. NORDHAUS - Institute for International Relations, 1989, Vietnam.

3- Currency and Bank – DANG CHI NHON, HO DIEU, Ph.D. NGO HUONG, Ph.D. DO LINH HIEP, Ph.D. LE VAN TE - Ho Chi Minh City Publishing House, 1992, Vietnam.

4 - Access to theories and monetary policy in a market economy. - TRUONG XUAN LE - Education Publishing House, 1993, Vietnam.

5- Use balance Money- Goods to eliminate inflation- NGUYEN CAO DUNG, Orient Publishing, 2005, Vietnam.

TABLE OF CONTENTS

www.ingramcontent.com/pod-product-compliance
Lightning Source LLC
Chambersburg PA
CBHW061217180526
45170CB00003B/1043

* 9 7 8 1 5 4 5 3 3 5 8 3 3 *